The

Wilted

Walls

Kristin L. Provenzano

The Wilted Walls

First published by
Magesoul Publishing

Formatted and edited by
Adric Ceneri

Cover design by
Magesoul Publishing

Published in the United States of America

To the man who has loved me unconditionally
My best friend
The first man to show me that not all men are bad out here
Who's hand was always waiting for mine
And would love when I would give him kisses
Who was always worried about me
When I didn't seem to worry about myself
That has had my heart since day one
Damn how much I miss you
And even though these tears continue to flow
My heart will always be full of the love I have for you
Thank you, grandpa,
For all of this
All these years
All these moments in time
And know at the end of my days
To the start of my mornings
You always will be the first and last on my mind

CONTENT

POEMS

You made me not like myself
I didn't want to look in the mirror anymore
I hated the person I saw in the reflection
Feeling like I was less than nothing
Maybe you were right

I remember a time when I had a smile on my face
Then you came around
And took it away

Same Line

And here it is again
Another tear
Believing another lie you told me
"This time it will be different"
But it's never different
Always the same line
You're down on your knees
Begging me to stay
I fall
You catch me
Like you're my hero
And just like that
Back to the same shit
Knocking me down farther
Until I'm drowning again
Then for time to repeat itself
Back to the same game
New day
But same line

Kristin L. Provenzano

Don't you get it
Possessions are replaceable
People aren't

Fuck

I'm just done
I'm fuckin done
As I scream
With tears running from my eyes
As I fall to my knees
Sobbing in my hands
Trying to catch my breath
I can't take this anymore
Fuck you for doing this to me
Fuck me for sticking around long enough
to endure this bullshit
I thought was love

You were nothing to me after a while
Because I was nothing to you
Since the day I was born

The Wilted Walls

Just like that
As soon as it began
It was over
Fuckin tragic
You lost someone who would of
never given up on you
That's what you failed to realize
Now all I see is the dust of how
quickly you left

3 a.m. wakeup call and it's you
You're drunk
Here I am with all these emotions again
I told myself so many times
I must keep you at a distance
For my heart is still attached to the taste of you
Why can't I just say no
You can't come over
Why is it that you have such a hold on me?
That the word no is impossible
What is it about you?
I can't stay away from
I rack my brain trying to figure this out
All I know is my life would seem sad without
you in it somehow
So, for now I guess
I'll take these 3 a.m. wake up calls
It still lets me know I'm on your mind

The Wilted Walls

I don't how fuckin people do it
They can just turn off their emotion
When they make a real connection
with someone
I get that people want to protect themselves
Protect their heart
But when someone comes along
Awakens something in you
You just can't turn that off so easily
Maybe I feel too much

When someone enters my life
And leaves an imprint on my soul
I can't push that away
Them or that feeling
But I would rather feel too much
Regardless of the outcome
We all need to feel and love
That out of pain will come beauty
To feel is to be alive

The Wilted Walls

When you left
I remember not wanting to wash my sheets
I just sat on my bed
Hugging that pillow you slept with
I could smell you
And damn that was a killer
I didn't want to wash away you
Wash away us
You smelled like home
And who wants to lose their home

Who I am when I'm with you

I don't want to fall back into that bottle
All it ever brought me was
More tears
Screaming
Lost nights
Rough mornings
I don't want to remember how it is
To take that last sip
To feel that last fall

The Wilted Walls

He knew what it was from the beginning
And played along as if he didn't see it coming
I wonder how many times he's been doing this
Which each heart he ended up tearing
Seems he mastered it
Though I would look over your shoulder
The hurt you put out will finds its way back
None of us are safe from pain

"I'm scared to have a voice"
They asked why
"Because every time I had one with him
He pounded me back into the ground
Leaving nothing but a trail of blood and bruises
Some strands of hair missing"
"Why don't you just leave him?"
The same question everyone asks
"Well the last time I tried to leave,
A broken rib came out of it
And he said the next time I would taste
the metal of the shovel"

The Wilted Walls

One more crack in this heart
You think I would be used to it by now
But each crack hurts just like the first

The sadistic shit people do
They say they love you
Then leave

The Wilted Walls

You only felt that way
After you got caught

As I started to build that wall up with you
I saw my heart turn into stone

What you expect people to do
What they usually do
Expectations
You usually get fucked in the end by both of them

Some days I tell myself I'm over you
Some days your face is the only thing I can see
I feel lost
Hoping
That you will reappear somehow
Tell me that you made a mistake
That we were meant to be
That you never want to be without me again

I do believe you cared about me
But I also believe
You cared about yourself more
And when it comes to a relationship
I will never be second best

The embarrassment of going to school
With a bruise on my face

The Cowards Way Out

Complete silence
After being told a number of fairy tales
He knew he could never make come true

Kristin L. Provenzano

Death is a horrible thing
It doesn't matter how long you knew the person
Death changes everyone
Sometimes we wish
We were the one who left
Because the pain is so unbearable

The Wilted Walls

I fell for it again
Those sweet words
I have heard many times over
The serpent can disguise itself so well

That's what he does
Coming through shredding hearts
With his machete
Until there's nothing left standing
But blood everywhere

The Wilted Walls

I saw a life with you
I saw me in the kitchen cooking
With a glass of red wine in my hand
You coming up while I sit on the counter
And you just giving me the sweetest kiss
That scene has played over in my mind many times
What a moment that could be for the both of us
I also saw us just sitting on the couch
Me in one of your shirt's
Figuring out what to watch
While I smile at just being in this moment with you
You gave me this warm feeling of you
just being my home
And when I think of your smile
Your smile makes me smile
There is just so much life behind it

See this is what I think about when I see a life with you
Doesn't matter where we go
Or what we do
As long as you're by my side
Is all I could ask for
That whatever comes our way
We both know we can face anything together
Maybe one day you will open up and see
this with me too
These moments don't come a lot in life
And when they appear
You want to hold on to it as tight as possible
I don't want us to be another love failed love story

Hole

Once again you left this gaping hole
in my heart
This time I don't think it will close up

God,
I didn't want to be that person who is heartless
Because I'm tired of a broken heart
But this last one just did it
Turning me into,
Cold
Ruthless
Not giving a fuck
Has clawed her way back in
The switch that turns off your emotions
Came down like a clap of thunder
And there was no turning back

The Wilted Walls

I shrunk back down to a size I didn't miss
That I vowed I would never go back to
But here it is
Another man
With ill intentions
And those words that cut like daggers

I wanted to fall down this time
Not get back up
Mentally it was like my brain was splattered
across the floor
Not sure how to recover from it all
Just a human shell
Of someone from the past

The Wilted Walls

I miss you
Even though I know you're
no good for me
Why is it
That our hearts
Always yearn for the ones who
could less for it
That will break it
Chew it up
Spit it out
We know there are good ones out there
But we choose to keep on going back to the pain
To the hurt
I guess it's a feeling we have come accustomed to
We would rather experience tears
Then smiles
Stress
Not joys
A cold shoulder
And not a warm hand

I just stayed staring at the wall
I really don't know how many days had passed
You were gone
I was stuck
Not knowing my next move
It was hard to turn away
Get back into a life without you
You were my home
Everything else crumbled around me
Except for this wall

The Wilted Walls

But it wasn't my fault
"That doesn't matter
You're here now
So, you can feel my wrath"

Echoes

I can't, I can't, I can't
This is it
Just stop
Leave
And never come back
I'm tired of it all
And I can't do this anymore
So please just go
Please
Go

The Wilted Walls

But the words never make it out of her mouth
She just sits there
Takes it all in
Continues to live in her silence
Pain
Agony
Regret
Denial
Sad, isn't it
We scream so loud in our heads
But for some reason the echoes never make it out

I can't breathe
And I won't last
I've fallen down these roads before
Can't escape my past

The Wilted Walls

It is sad
Once nonstop calls and texts
Turns into silence
When your favorite thing was to see their name
appear on your phone
Has taken a step back
And lost its momentum
You try and rack your brain
Coming up with so many scenarios
On how something so good
Seemed to go so wrong
Now all that is left is
What if's and what could have been

The silence can be a killer
Draining you completely
Turning your whole world around
All I can say is
Be strong
Stay true
And know at the end of the night
You tried to do everything right
But sometimes life is here to teach us
Not everyone we think is right for us
Is right for us at this time

The Wilted Walls

People wonder
Why other people's hearts turn black
It has been burned
Too many times
To beat life back into it

I never wanted to let you go
But you seemed fine with losing grip on me

Thoughts of the morning

Sometimes it does hurt
I wake up in the morning
And you're still the first thing on my mind
Oh, how I wish you were just a dream
Just to know that none of it was real
It was at our fingertips
Now I'm just left in the shadows
Trying to figure how to get back to "us"
My heart still whispers your name
Though my mind tries to silence it
My heart breaks through every time
It doesn't want to give up
Neither do I

Doesn't matter how old you get
The lies still seem to trickle out of your mouth

The Wilted Walls

I never knew why I wasn't good enough for you

Why you wanted to tear me down
To forget who I am?
Maybe you like the high of conquering
Or maybe you got off on the control

The Wilted Walls

I cut out my heart
It got tired of bleeding from other people

The fact that I would rather be black out
drunk every weekend
Then deal with my reality
Because it seemed alcohol was the only one there for me
Not you

The Wilted Walls

Our love was like a rose with its thorns

Heartache
Some tears
And
A glass of red wine

Empty

As the light crept through my curtain
And laid flat on my bed
The silence entered that you're not here
As I slid my hand across that spot
And for the first time
I could feel how empty my room was

I couldn't control it anymore
I had to scream
You fucked me up
Now I'm left to deal with the aftermath

Didn't Realize

And then the tears poured out like waterfalls
I never knew someone could create this
many tears with such few words
Felt like my heart stopped
I needed to reach up for a breath
But sadly, couldn't find any
At the time you feel hopeless
I mean I feel hopeless
You care for someone
And then for it to get ripped away is tragic
The one you lay next to at night
That holds your hand while slowly falling asleep

Those small things are what makes the pain worse
I think those are the things that mess with you the most
You're a prisoner in your own head and thoughts
Wishing just for a call or text
To know that they are thinking about you
as much as them
That's what we wish for when that person is not around
Funny thing I never knew about this is
I didn't realize I was in love until now
The moment it got taken away

The Wilted Walls

I don't know what is worse
Drowning in tears
Or drowning in a bottle

I finally had to tell myself to tell you
goodbye on the inside
Didn't matter how much I wanted you in my life
I saw the feelings weren't reciprocated
How much that killed me
I had to let you go
With that last tear streaming down my cheek for you

The Wilted Walls

All that was left was
Empty bottles
Cigarette butts
And a tear-soaked pillow

Kristin L. Provenzano

I didn't realize how much of a number he did on me
Until I left

The Wilted Walls

Oh yeah
The pain is there
I can feel it
Like a knife piercing my skin
I forgot about how this felt
It's been so long since someone woke up
up my soul
And now the pain I dreaded so much
Has slowly crept back in
Making it hard to even think
Let alone the sadness that reappears
Why is it that this pain has such a hold on us at times?
Your soul feels like there is a chip in it
Yes, that's it
Your soul has been chipped a little each time
this pain reenters
We stitch it back up
As best as we can

Knowing that any time after you're healed from it
There is a chance for it to come back
Now do we take that chance with another
To give them the power
That they hold something in the end
That could cause another chip in our soul
Or should we just shut off our emotions
Having a wall so high
You would never be able to get over it
But what about the true believers in love
The ones who know they could get hurt every time
They still know and believe
There is that one person out there for them
That as many times as the pain has come back
Or will continue to come back

The Wilted Walls

It will be all worth it in the end
Because what's waiting for us
Was worth all the pain
Every tear shed
And many of sleepless nights
That the outcome will be one of greatest joys we could ever
feel
I'll take that chance every time
Because I am one of those people
Love is such a powerful thing
And something with that much power
Has its way of finding exactly where it needs to be

I wonder if every time someone
breaks your heart
It sheds a layer
Until there's nothing left
But a shell of what it used to be

Why a man chooses to raise his hand to a
woman
I will never understand
And I never want to be inside of the head
of someone like that

He heard me cry
I don't know how many times
But his reaction was just to sit there and listen
He would rather have tears flow out of my eyes
Then to wipe them away
Heartbreaking to say the least

The Wilted Walls

You have to open up to me a little bit
You can't completely shut me out when life
gets tough
Then there is no point in having a relationship
with someone
Because if I can't help you at your lowest
If you don't want me there
I shouldn't be around you
The only thing I know how to do
Is to show love to the people I care about
To help lift them up when they feel like there is no air
And breathe life back into them
That's the only way I know how to be

If that is to "real" for you
Or if you don't want someone like this in your life
I will leave
How much it might break me
I will do it
No one likes to feel that they are standing
on the edge of a cliff
So, will you catch me if I fall?
And if not
Let me land on my feet
To walk away

The Wilted Walls

He told me I'm useless
What am I good for?
I started to believe it

Self- destructing

Cheap men
Cheap booze
Cheap cigarettes
Smeared eye makeup

The Wilted Walls

Tormented by thoughts of us
Staring down at the end of the glass
Wearing your sweatshirt
I can still smell your scent
Your set of keys on the table

For a while
I felt bad for you
Felt bad about your past relationship
How that girl hurt you
Made you lose faith in a good woman being out there
How she made you not want to trust anyone again
But then I started to see a side of you I didn't think was there
You claimed to not be like the rest
You would be honest
Forthcoming
With anything that was happening between us
You know I do understand hurt
Tears that have soaked pillows
Where you are so in your head
That you can't get out of it
I was open with you about me

The Wilted Walls

You never had to wonder what my intentions were
Where I stood
I mean someone who has experienced pain
Would never want to inflict that on anyone else right?
Maybe you're too damaged on the inside to care
about how you treat others
I don't know
But I refuse to let anyone use their past pain as an excuse in
the poor treatment of others around them
So, take you
Your baggage
Your hurtful ways
They are not wanted here
And as sad as I might be to see you go
I will not be a punching bag in someone's life

You made me believe your words
All that is left is your words

Trapped inside my head
You never deserved a heart like mine
in your life

Sometimes the hardest part of it all
Is when you have to pick yourself up
All by yourself

To a Conversation We Will Probably Never Have

I was thinking for while
Maybe this could be it
I was holding onto that hope
Because I could picture parts of my life with you
I wanted it to be like that so bad
I didn't want to look for anyone else
I only wanted to look at you
But after you didn't reach out
Or even respond
And you just left me standing there alone
What was I supposed to do?
Just stay standing there.
I realized I had to let you go
As hard as that was
So, I shut you out completely
Blocking you from any form in my life
Because I wanted my time to heal
I deserved that

I don't care if you don't get why I did what I did
This is my life
Not yours
And honestly
I was ready to forgive you for the hurt you caused me
I really was
I wanted
No, I need that part of my life back
Where I could wake up with a smile again
An honest smile of no bullshit
Once you experience peace in your life
It becomes addicting
It makes you confront anything that disturbs it
To deal with it
And move on
So that's what I did
There are no regrets with you
You taught me a lesson
Of having someone fight for me
That I am as important as the other

The Wilted Walls

I deserve that effort too
Thank you for that
Really
It has been a blessing in disguise
A lesson well leaned
So, know when I say this
I wish the best for you
I hope you learn from us
And whoever may come along in your life later
Treat them as you would want to be treated
There are two people in a relationship
Not just one

Holding onto you
Was like holding onto a razor blade

Learn

The sad part
We just learn to live without people

Nighttime is the worst
That's when everything comes out
Flashbacks of
Smiles
Laughter
Tears
Hope
Hopelessness
Why's
Pain
Heartache
Spinning out of our mind
Taste of the kiss
Anticipation
Let down
Lost
Alone
Staring at nothing
Wishing
And realization
Nighttime damns us
Keeping us awake
Feeling everything, we try so much to deny

Those invisible scars
No one knows about

I didn't want to let you go
I wanted you here by my side
Why does life have this timing
In the moments where you never want them to end
When the last thing I saw
Was your hand leaving mine
Now I'm all alone
Feeling nothing
Stuck
Desperately wanting to relive you
Again, and again

The Wilted Walls

I wanted to lock myself away
Not be around anyone
I was tired of putting on this façade
Truth was I wasn't ok
Mentally I was fucked up

Me bouncing off the bed
But for some reason
I couldn't feel your hits to my face
Weird
A time I will always remember
Then mom entered
She was always my angel
Stopping the pain
Putting herself in the way

The Wilted Walls

Still to this day
When I think you have changed for the better
You prove me wrong

I tried to stop you from leaving
But you just threw me on the ground
Showing me
I should have been the first one to leave

The Wilted Walls

Everything has been grey for so long
That a little pop of color frightened me
Somehow,
I became content with living in the gloom

You know I always wanted him to care
Go on family vacations with us
Dinners
But he was the most important one in his life
So, there is no pictures with him in it
Just the memories of a ghost

The Wilted Walls

After all of the bottles I have taken down
I could fill each one of them up
With my tears

Some pain is just too hard
To wash away

The Wilted Walls

While I'm over here thinking about you
You were over there thinking about nothing
While I'm over here shedding tears over you
You're over there smiling through your day
While I'm over here willing to stand by your side through
anything
You were over there making up scenarios in your head
on what could happen
While I'm over here having my heart break
You were over there acting like I was nothing
While I'm over thinking you meant everything you said
You were over there spitting your lies
Now I'm just stuck at damn over here

I camouflaged everything on me
This heart
These feelings
I was tired of the hurt
Over the stress
Pain
So, to protect myself
I took away the appearance of giving a fuck
That was the only way I knew how to survive

The Wilted Walls

"You're killing me" she said
He couldn't understand why
Until one day
All that sat in front of him
Was this decimated woman he used to know
And then he realized
He was her disease

I'm scared for my heart to get attached to you
Because the last time
That other person
Fuckin cut that shit out of my chest
Tossed away
Like it wasn't shit

The Wilted Walls

You say you like me
But what I was asking for was a "bit much"
Why is that?
Because I required the bare minimum from you
And I got vocal about it
When I was tired of not getting it
But it was ok for you to come and say sorry how many times
That you were "just all over the place"
And I accepted each apology
Knowing that life happens
Still welcoming you in my life
All I wanted was a little more effort
Some phone calls here and there
I mean, damn
That's all I was asking for
And you tell me "that's a bit much"

Who told you how relationships were supposed to be?
That it's all about you?
No, sweetheart,
It's not
You met a real woman
Who was also looking for something
What you also claimed to be looking for
I'm not sorry for telling you I wasn't feeling appreciated
And I was tired of waiting for your calls when you said
you were going to call
My time is just as important as yours
So I'll be damned if a man is going to make me
feel some type of way because I was honest
Who the hell are you to tell me anything else?
And really you knew all along you weren't treating me right
Because there never would been an apology the first time

I forgot who I was for so long
That I cried it ever had to come to that

When you get to the point where you feel like you're worthless
Nothing else matters

You think I like being inside my head tormenting myself?
But that's what anxiety will do
Creates the worst situations
Making it bleed profusely
Draining you completely

Kristin L. Provenzano

I don't want to let you go
But I can't keep on fighting this war alone

The Wilted Walls

All I seen was black
I fell hard into that hole
That dirt piling up
With my last breath exhaled

Even though I haven't heard from you
I still think about you every day
Maybe not as many times in those days as
it used to be
But you're still on my mind
Sometimes I go and look at pictures of you
And I think what could of have been
My heart misses yours
I really don't know where it all went wrong
But I knew I wanted to be in it for the long haul
I saw something in us
That it looked like we could finally stop searching
As soon as it began
It was over
How sad
I may never find out the reason why
But at this point do I want to know
I'm not sure of that anymore
That's ok I guess

The Wilted Walls

These four walls
Have seen
And heard so much

Kristin L. Provenzano

ABOUT THE AUTHOR

Kristin Provenzano was born and raised in Akron, Ohio. She started writing at a young age and had her
first poem published in high school. Kristin started really falling into poetry because some of the toxic
relationships she had been in over the years. That inspired her to write about what she has gone though
and in hopes will help people deal with what they have been through. To show they are not alone in this
world. Kristin wants people to realize its ok to talk about what has happened in their life. That we are all
in this together.

Kristin L. Provenzano

Connect with the author on social media

Instagram: @kristin_l_provenzano

Facebook: @kristinprovenzano

Twitter: @provenzanokris1

Coming Soon by
MAGESOUL PUBLISHING

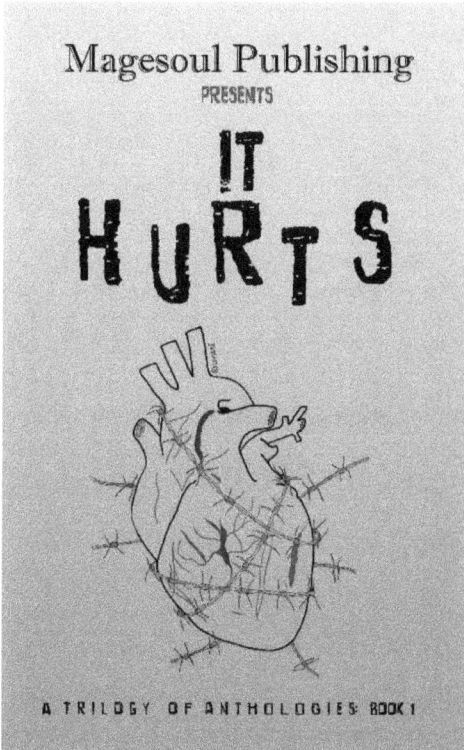

Magesoul Publishing
PRESENTS

IT
HURTS

A TRILOGY OF ANTHOLOGIES BOOK 1

Available on MARCH 15 2020

Coming Soon by
MAGESOUL PUBLISHING

MAGESOUL PUBLISHING
PRESENTS

DETOURS

Anthology Vol 1

Leaving marks on every
path we take in life

Available on SUMMER 2020